Journeys Through Prairie and Forest

Poetic Essays On the Big Questions of Life

Volume 7 — Time and Space, Awesome Teachers

Journeys Through Prairie and Forest

Poetic Essays On the Big Questions of Life

Volume 7 — Time and Space, Awesome Teachers

Volume Seven of a Seven-Volume Set

By Paul W. Syltie

Also by Paul W. Syltie

The Syltie Family in America

The New Eden: Millennial Agriculture,
a Key to Understanding the Kingdom of God

How Soils Work: a Study Into the God-Plane
Mutualism of Soils and Crops

Understanding God's Government,
With Contrasts to Satan's Governmental System

The Three Edens, the Story of God's Universe, Earth,
and Mankind in Conflict With the Adversary

Pathways to Joy in Marriage;
Live This Way and Happiness Will Pursue You!

The Bridge to Eden, the Arduous Passage
From This Age of Chaos to the Next Age of Perfection

Journeys Through Prairie and Forest
Volume 7. Time and Space, Awesome Teachers
by Paul W. Syltie

Publisher: IngramSpark
Copyright © 2020 by Paul W. Syltie
Editor: Paul Syltie
Editorial Assistant/Proofreader: Sandy Syltie
Photographer: Paul Syltie
Interior Design/Composition: Greg Smith
Cover Design: Greg Smith

NOTICE OF RIGHTS

All rights reserved solely by the author. The author guarantees all contents are original and do not infringe upon the legal rights of any other person or work. No part of this book may be reproduced in any form without the permission of the author. The views expressed in this book are not necessarily those of the publisher.

ISBN-978-0-9980254-6-9

Printed in the United States of America

To my wonderful wife of 53 years,
and to our children and grandchildren who are the hope of the future.

Table of CONTENTS Volume 7

Preface   VIII
Chapter 1   Aging...1
Chapter 2   Born Out of Time...10
Chapter 3   Entropy...13
Chapter 4   Eternity...17
Chapter 5   Future...28
Chapter 6   Patience...30
Chapter 7   Perfection Over Time...37
Chapter 8   Passing of Time...38
Chapter 9   Use of Time...46
Chapter 10   Take Careful Note of the Beauty Within Your Space...52

All photos have been taken by the author over many years.

PREFACE

WHO AM I?
WHY AM I HERE?
WHAT IS MY DESTINY?

These three questions have haunted the lives of virtually every thinking person on earth to one degree or another. They point to the very heart of our existence, and to our ultimate value, our worthiness to exist. Are we products of evolution from a primordial sea-soup, without any defined purpose in being here, or are we creations in the image of a Creator whose plan for us transcends our understanding?

The answers to these simple but profound questions dictate our decisions day by day, and ultimately the course of our careers, our friendships, our marriage partners, and how we interact within our families and communities. In many ways these answers direct our career pathway through life, and most assuredly influence our joy and fulfillment in everyday living.

I am stepping out by claiming that I have found answers — sound answers — to all three of these questions, and I am audacious enough to suggest that they are correct answers. They agree with what I understand is Truth, which is rooted in the great eternal God who made all things, and who sustains all things through the Word of His power and revelation.

But there the simplicity ends. My audacity has led to great conflicts with the realities of a corrupted earth and universe … a corrupted human race that clings to existence day-by-day upon the whims of weather and cooperation … neither of which often prosper to any race's benefit. We are always only weeks away from famine upon an earth that so often insults the farmer and gardener with drought, floods, heat, frost, or tempest.

As a farm boy raised close to nature, I have been so often forced from my peaceful home into the prairies and forests, the lakes, streams, and oceans of this wide earth to regain my bearings, to restore hope and gratitude, and to reset the pathway ahead when darkness threatens to overwhelm me. To leave the sterile unease of concrete jungles and flee to the forests and prairies of sanity has become a habit over the years — an addiction, one might say — and with that flight has emerged a continued stream of verbal expression that has leaped from my fingers. I cannot explain why, just that I must do it.

So … here is a collection of some of those writings expounded over the years, some of them clearly poetic, and some of them bordering more on short essays. I attempted some way to categorize them to make them flow, but they have defied clear organization; each item is too complex to easily arrange in a coherent order. Thus, I have let them fall where they may within broad categories, and have applied pictures I have taken through the years to emphasize the messages. Photographing nature has been a passion much of my life; these images speak louder and more eloquently than my words.

I hope you enjoy these messages, and are brought into a closer association with the Creator as a result so you will be able to answer these three big questions a bit better yourself. Let us walk together through the prairies and forests of our land, our beautiful, God-given land that speaks to us so eloquently if we will but open our ears and listen.

Aging

Chapter 1

Age

I met a nice man of gray hair and his wife,
Whose ages looked certainly twice of my life.
But then he said gravely to my great dismay
That both of us shared the same birthday!
Then in silence I pondered the depth of abuse
That style of one's living can annihilate youth.

Aging

As soon as things are made new in this dim age of wasting,
They lose their luster, fade and break … the fate of nature hasting.

Change

Life to life, age to age, growing older stage by stage;
Knowing not the next event, fleeting youth its style be spent.
Hope abounding, plans be laid, joy's accomplishment be paid,
While we labor to be master of our selves forever after.
Yet so fickle lay our nature bound in bonds of fleshly pleasure,
That our life from age to age must seek that source of wisdom sage.

Galapagos Islands, Ecuador. *Showing the character of seemingly ancient life forms, the giant tortoises of the Galapagos Islands still survive quite well despite their ponderous, cumbrous nature, and commonly reach the age of several hundred years.*

Canby, Minnesota.
The love of a grandfather for his granddaughter is the stuff that makes life worthwhile for the aged, as well as for the younger generation that dwells upon the fact that this beloved progenitor will not be around too much longer … but in the meantime can teach so much from an abundance of experience.

JOURNEYS THROUGH PRAIRIE AND FOREST Poetic Essays On The Big Questions of Life

Aging

House Aflame

I built my house on a foundation of Rock,
At first of wood …

> But it burned up amidst the heat of the day.

Then rarer metals I tried, a bit of gold and silver with the wood.
As the years passed quickly, from youth to teen,

> All but the gold and silver burned, blackened to ash.
> Then the walls caved in … yet there stood an open door.

Childhood faded, manhood commenced, and sounder the house was built,
A dwelling of precious stones — agates, amethysts, rubies, jade —

> Which stood up solidly while fires flew against its gleaming walls,
> Flames licking clean the paper, wood, and chaff remaining.

Onward marched adult years as fleeting as light,
The house furnished this way and that, some yet of straw and wood,
   some of precious things,

> And fires came again and again,
>   Charring, consuming the hapless combustibles to nothing … painfully
>   but quickly.

I now stand firmly upon the Rock, the true Foundation,
Amidst fiery trials that ever beset this house,
Ever purifying, leaving it never furbished quite the same.

Chapter 1 Aging

Take Heed of Time

"Time, how short its life," the young man said,
While lying sick upon his own death bed.
"I wish the trails had led this way or that,
Instead of here or there; oh bring them back!"

But death ruled first and cut his tenure short,
As mothers, friends bemoaned this sad report.
Now trails led six feet down, that's not so strange,
And there at last report they've never changed.

The Author of Life

Time slips by so quietly, serenely,
I scarcely note her passing …
And perspectives on life change ever so steadily
I hardly sense the shift
That each new day so deftly sifts to the next …
A creature yet exploring meanings of things,
Yet never capturing the elusive pattern
Of human patchwork experience
Woven intricately into schemes
Only the Creator can author.

Yellowstone National Park, Wyoming. *A grizzled old bison bull has stood the tests of harsh mountain cold and blizzards, grizzly bears and cougars, rival males and disease, and sheds its winter coat in preparation for yet another oncoming winter. Aging creates stamina amongst nature's creatures to be able to bear up to the elements thrown at them.*

VOLUME 7. Time and Space, Awesome Teachers 5

Aging — Chapter 1

The Path

The Father's sons know not the path
Their feet must tread in life-long course,
But seek the way — so plain and firm —
Our Savior trod, without remorse.

We know not how or why this path
So deftly winds through field and forest,
Often overgrown by briars,
Fraught by fearful lion's chorus.

Swiftly flow the days of life
Upon earth's troubled face resilient,
Paths converging from all quarters
Onto one grand highway brilliant.

Here I stand, in latter days,
Content where journey's way shall send,
Nor desire to stem the course,
Heavenly light at pathway's end.

Tucson, Arizona. *While the earth has endured many changes and crises through the eons, worldwide floods millennia ago have preserved evidence of creatures that look very much like those we see on land and in the oceans today. The earth has aged, but its rock strata have preserved a remarkable record of the creatures that once teemed upon its face.*

Aging

What Lasts?

We men of flesh live lives of fervent, prescient agony,
Groping through the jagged reefs, unmarked through churning seas,
Unfit to leave one's legacy, short respite on the earth,
Hindered by our fleshly temples, slinking slow towards death.

We blossom for a moment, then release this brief existence,
Watching with unfolding awe our slide to non-persistence,
Recalling that our only hope lies planted 'midst the plain
Of God's eternal spirit life: there shall our mark remain.

Vietnam.
Bending as a willow towards the earth, tropical cactus flowers show forth a beauty that renews itself each new season, reminding us that though the earth grows old, its awesome creations revive its aging face time after time.

Chapter 2 Born Out of Time

Born Out of Time

A pioneer of Eden, born out of time,
Servant of the Eternal, sanctified, sublime,
I know not why, yet captured to service
Of soil, tree, and herb, resplendent purpose
Beyond time's dimension.

Removed from lands fair, fertile and vital …
From fathers and mothers, families and idols
To lands strange and foreboding, foretelling in loneliness
This soul's fresh vision to conquer with holiness
Lost mansion's dwelling.

Given instead those lands lost in youth,
Fathers and mothers, strong kin brave and couth,
And into bright futures this land has been won
For one undeserving as this loyal son,
Youth's hopes renewed.

British Columbia, Canada. *As if heralding the message of release from bondage to a new Eden to be thrust across the earth, white foxgloves trumpet forth their beauty for all to see … if they will but look. They, like us, preach a message of hope for a much better world once this thralldom to decay is overturned.*

Entropy

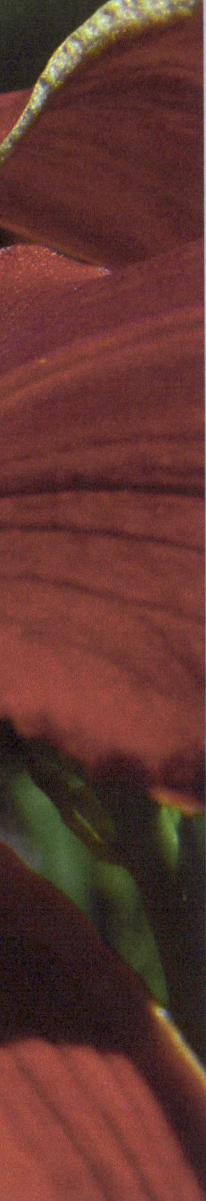

Entropy

Entropy functions in all,
Human systems of machinery and vice bound to tumble
As laws ancient exact their toll
Upon the disobedient in their short-sighted plunder
Of the nature meant to serve and support them.

Down, down tumbles Babylon, the mystery of ages past,
Forgotten in one generation in her creation — the nations obsessed with
    her carnal, crimson robes.
Forgotten in a generation after her demise,
She cannot endure,
For her author must reap his just due,
And fall headlong into the abyss.

The system struggles to progress, provide — in vain —
Doves, deer, bass, tender lilies, man himself falling headlong beneath the
    writhing monster of carnal materialistic gain,
Heated adultery, injustice, love of money, hedonistic reveling, drunkenness
    … lust for sensuality and love of self.

Continued on page 14

Morris, Minnesota. *While all energy tends to run downhill towards disorder and randomness within a closed thermodynamic system, in the physical world as well as in the societies of men that operate apart from the Creator's laws, yet the upbuilding powers of life reverse the process and, like a beautiful lily, bring order and stability to an otherwise decrepit and unlivable landscape.*

Chapter 3: Entropy

Continued from page 13

    Unseen of mind they exact the toll.
    Gravity holds her victim's feet to the earth,
    Inertia and momentum hold planets and galaxies in orbit,
        electrons captive to nuclei,
    And love must conquer hate, impatience, harshness, injustice;
    Gratitude and forgiveness, the gems of peaceful living,
        must slay unthankfulness and deceit.

    Entropy exacts its toll on man.
    Laws immutable must be lovingly cultured, or break the lawbreaker.
    What is the essence of all? Obey God, do His will,
        and serve Him only in all things,
    For entropy leads to eternity, the hope of all men,
        the everlasting life to come.

    Bring it soon, my Father, and Your Son, my Brother at Your right hand!

Sinai, South Dakota. *The moon in its orbit around the earth reveals the awesome forces that give order to all of the cosmos, forces that over time degenerate into disorder... reminding us of the imperative need for a regeneration of all things that is promised to come.*

Eternity

Time

Time, that essence of being,
With space its consort
Defines what was,
And is, and is to come,
The I AM.

New Zealand. *A silver fern creates the Fibonacci golden ratio in an elegant spiral, typical of the 1.618 vortex mean found throughout the earth and all of the universe, a spiritual dynamic tied to eternity past and future and offering glimpses into the creative designs of the Eternal.*

Eternity

Chapter 4

Life in a Moment

I am but a child of the Maker's hand, of clay,
Plagued by the shame of flesh in its decay,
Longing in tear-filled hope for the moment
When finally the flesh is suddenly changed
To that everlasting new body of spirit.
Is it not so interesting then, so exciting,
That for just one moment — not really time at all —
I commit the full intent of this life,
To infinite bits of obedience to the Maker's mind?

Outside of Time

Flying through space, unnaturally so, God's heaven mirrored
Through spacious seas, billowing clouds, azure tholos,
Thrusting timeless imagination into fancy's lost domain,
Recalling lost realms still unseen, yet vividly real
In which I reside.

Italy. *Marvelous structures built by man, most of them dating back centuries if not millennia, such as Stonehenge, Mayan temples, the Great Pyramid, and cathedrals from the Middle Ages, contain dimensions that reveal the builders' knowledge of mathematics and geometry that point towards the Creator's eternal truths.*

Sinai, South Dakota. *Even the seeds of an opening milkweed pod reveal the order and dimensions that only the Creator could design. Row upon row of vibrantly alive seeds, made in the image of the heavenly, lie ready to be wafted up by the wind to seek an acceptable growing environment as the plan of the Designer is to continue expanding and increasing His realm without end.*

Eternity

Ranging Long

I know not what this life may bring.
Tomorrow lies sequestered deep within the folds of this southerly wind
Caressing my suntanned face, rustling the grass pointing heavenward,
Rushing through grizzled oaks and supple basswoods,
Warblers hidden amongst the deep-green leaves of stately ash and elms.
Sixty years have passed since first my cry announced to earth another
    soul had arrived,
Now set here amongst the early summer flowers and rushing brooks of
    creation's mysteries …
Eyes ever searching for bits of beauty within niches consigned to decay,
    depravity, ugliness,
Things that I comprehend beyond the simple truths cast before restless,
    wayward crowds.
I cannot fathom what this hand must do to share its God-plane wisdom yet beyond
The monuments of earth sublime.
I must rely on truths so firmly planted even before my birth,
Those wistful whispers welling up within my bosom day by day,
Beyond understanding, beyond man's knowing,
Cast by the Creator upon this miry clay, formed to fit his aged plans
Beyond the refined senses of inquisitive servants.
I shall not rest until those senses are richly blessed within this life of
    flowering revelation,
That hope may spring forth forever blessed upon this hard-pressed seeking soul,
Whose quests fill ageless prophets' breasts.

Chapter 4 Eternity

This I Crave

As years roll by, relentlessly witnessed
Amongst life's profound realities,
I discover the things called "great" in history
Now shine less illustriously than they did …
But now the profound virtues of eternity
Of foreverness, tomorrow's hope, this soul esteems …
Seas of enlightenment confounding passing fads of history,
With temporal values rightfully tossed overboard,
Left to drift and fade into distance's foggy abyss.
What shall last forever is what I crave;
All else fades into death's darkened grave.

Where I Am

Self bound by flesh speaks softly through the gray
And misty realm of three dimension's sway;
Yet set within some space lies deeper grace,
Wherein this spirit rests … appointed place.

Italy. *It has been the goal of many people to achieve immortality, ever since Adam and Eve sinned in the Garden of Eden and faced certain death… death that passed down to all mankind. This zeal towards eternal life can be seen in the many stone carvings seen in museums in many countries… but even stone erodes and turns to dust. Eternity can be only through the Creator and His great plan for us.*

Eternity

Chapter 4

The Vineyard

I walked carefully through the wet, supple grass this morning,
Storms having drenched the land once again after winter's hard frosts and blizzards.
Rested and restored I was after week's challenges, fears, and oppressions,
As liberty I sought ... and now found in this day of renewal.

The vines I had been carefully watching after the deep snow had finally vanished
    and slunk into the rich black soil;
Surely they are dead, so lifeless, gray and shaggy with splitting bark after the horribly
    cold days and nights of this past especially cruel winter.
Surely the insults during their icy slumber had left them helpless victims of merciless
    frigid, whipping winds.
They stood as barren sentinels of death above the lush green grass,
    trailing vines useless and drab, ready for the burn pile.

So this morning I slowly strolled to the vineyard, hoping for some sort of surprise
    from these ailing branches.
Reaching them, I looked, and what did I see, but healthy, robust buds
    reaching out to me!
Their green, supple buds peeked out of the craggy vines of dark gray, shredded bark,
Some yet tiny, but others unfurling their new-found life appearing like hands in prayer,
    saying to me, "Look, we live!"

Continued on page 26

Sinai, South Dakota. *From vines and branches that seem dead from winter's harsh cold, tender, supple shoots miraculously emerge from tiny buds amidst the grays and browns of winter's slumber. How this is possible remains a giant mystery that we can only describe in scientific terms, or through the awesome words of the Creator, whose skillful hands made the entire earth bring forth abundantly the sustenance of man.*

Chapter 4 Eternity

Continued from page 25

    Even the lower branches trailing along the wire guides, seemingly hopelessly
        lifeless few days ago,
    Had begun to sprout forth tiny, white buds through the blackened bark.
    I could not believe the scene before my eyes: the whole vineyard was alive,
        whereas before it was dead!
    Up and down the rows shot forth buds — some barely visible,
        some already opening — praising life renewed, the living emerging from
        the death of winter's depths!

    Tears came to my eyes: what messages to behold …
    The vineyard of all mankind on display before me.
    Israel and gentile nations alike had lost their way, gone to sleep in an icy winter
        of ignorance and depravity,
    Their buds of life lost amongst the blackened bark of the parent vine
        that looked dead … but was not.

    It was the Living Vine that no one recognized, not of comely features so one
        would desire Him.
    Those buds of life — oh how could they ever revive? — seemed stricken
        hopelessly in captivity, asleep within the craggy bark,
    Yet crying in spirit for release from their mortal captivity,
    Seeking emergence from that seemed to be an eternal grave, but now suddenly
        given opportunity for life!

    All of the Creator's vineyard stood before me, those magnificent miracles
        made in His image,
    Reaching out from the death of slavery's winter into life … life abundant,
        without sorrow and without end,
    Glorious cells of life multiplying vigorously in springtime's warming days,
        nourishing rains, and balmy sunshine,
    Proclaiming liberty throughout the land, joy erupting from the chorus of countless
        images of the Godly emerging from their cocoons of silence.

Continued on page 27

Eternity — Chapter 4

Continued from page 26

Then my eyes caught sight of a trailing branch.
It looked dead like the others, but this one was markedly shriveled and dry,
   and not one bud appeared along its darkened bark.
My heart sank as I viewed the death of this lifeless vine,
And I prayed that somehow it might image the heavenly and not be lost ... be liberated
   from its captivity to the adversary's lies, and live.

Suddenly appeared two brilliantly yellow goldfinches upon the budding vines,
Lively and exuberant, flitting from branch to branch, singing their virtuoso melodies
   amidst the bursting life of a trillion dividing and swelling cells,
Like angels encouraging the buds to flourish into gorgeous, beautiful, row-shrouding
   canopies of florid vines,
Fluttering in the spirit winds of the Creator's eternal joy alongside New Jerusalem's
   sparkling crystal waters and trees of life,
Bearing the deep-purple fruit of the True Vine, sweet and tasty beyond compare,

Having within them the seeds of new life, new vines to seed the earth and then all the
   universe
With vineyards yielding fruit of joy and peace never-ending ... to the end of time.

Chapter 5 Future

Future

To ride majestically upon a fleecy fall cloud, amid the blue viewed through tattered edges of wispy white,
Free to view with soaring spirits the good earth below, its fertile, bountiful black blanket nourishing towering forests and endless grasslands …
As mightily the rushing wind would speed — unhindered by blight of man — the shadow beneath playing tag with birds and beasts …
And men, women, children — knit in oneness with warmth— would shed no tears, nor fear hurt feelings … what a boundless quest.
Release the cottony fluffs above to cascade quietly, serenely upon the warming sun,
The helper of life, love … the forgiver of loneliness and poverty.
Browns and yellows among winter's fields cannot undo the vibrant anticipation of springtime warming, fragrant breezes,
When geese and ducks will fill the air with their melodious chorus, among these very clouds, swept northward with anticipation of summer;
When hope becomes reality and destiny blends with infinity.

Sinai, South Dakota. *A fall of fresh snow upon emerging tulips cannot thwart the oncoming springtime warmth, as the procession of the seasons relentlessly brings on the beauty and increase of fields and forests, and the plants, animals, birds, insects, and other creatures that inhabit them … always pressing forward towards the increase and prosperity of their own kind.*

Chapter 6. Patience

Blessed ... Not Yet

I have reaped things I never hoped or dreamed for, or planted,
But have been granted those things freely by the One who desired them for me.
Of all creatures on earth I am most richly blessed.
In a season those heaven-sent dreams borne from my youth
Shall become reality — in due time —
And the tender and keeper that I am will be expressed
Within a land of great abundance ...
For all time.

Slow Down, My Soul

Slow down your life, and let visions be exalted through lenses of patience.
Let fleecy bright cumulus roll and cavort across the heavens of your soul,
Bearing up all burdens brightly on eagle's wings,
Restoring the dreams and hopes of lives submerged in the swirling whirlpools
Of insane culture adrift on a sea of haste.

China. *The Chinese have farmed the same rice paddies in some cases for about 4,000 years, and the productivity of the crop is still superb, even with the same ancient animal power as used centuries before. The patient, longsuffering labor of the farmer and the ox has brought life to countless generations, even as patient attention to the tasks at hand brings triumph in our ventures.*

VOLUME 7. Time and Space, Awesome Teachers

Patience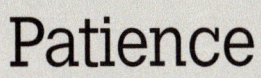

Time in Conflict

Some days life drags by like a snail,
Imagination never sets sail.
I find the course in wheel-tracks fits
To paralyze sublime mind bits.

Were things made simple I would cry
And sweat 'till ventures reached the sky,
But simple days shall never unfold
As brothers' hands in need I hold.

Time Slipping

Time, time, you slip away, so subtly, so softly.
Like a cat creeping stealthily through the night you slip away.
All my days seem filled with tears and sorrow,
But onward I travel … for time will not cease for this creature
Before my quotas are full.

Zimbabwe. *The waters on the earth evaporate from lakes and oceans, the wind carries the vapor over land, and there some of it precipitates to water the plants that sustain the lives of mankind and beasts. The cyclical process is endless, and expresses the great patience of the systems that the Creator has in place to bless and multiply all living things He has made.*

Chapter 6 Patience

Time's Awesome Gift

Grant me the tools to work,
And in great efforts shall I lift
Strong hands to heal earth's face,
Make it a better place.
But alas, where lie these wares?
When shall my soul its prayers
In answers reach the lofty height
Through unimpeded deeds done right?
A voice speaks softly through the night:
"Great patience around you lurks;
You know not time's awesome gift."

California. *There is no better resource to build than the soil that feeds us. It is the very substance of life, that grows the crops which feed and cloth us… but building soil to a high level of fertility takes time. The farmer must patiently excercise his tools of returning organic residues, fertilizing, and preventing erosion, just as we must build the soil of our personal lives to grow into the productive plants of our Creator's garden.*

Perfection Over Time

Day Upon Day

We change ever so slightly each day,
Imperceptibly,
But count the days of such change
And add them together ...
Day upon day, line upon line —
A vessel of worth created from a heap of refuse,
A sparkling gem from a rugged ugly rock ...
A stunning temple from a house of straw.

Sinai, South Dakota. *We can never achieve perfection in this world, but we do the best we can through the power of the spirit dwelling within us ... like a plain stone that shows no character or beauty until it is cut and polished to expose the incredible elegance within.*

Chapter 8 Passing of Time

Flight of Time

Consider the days
How quickly they flee …
One glance, one gaze
Far horizons to see,
While footsteps adroitly
Seek steppingstones firm …
Life not too politely
Upending square terms.

    Sea upon sea,
    Upon bended knee
    Search out the morrow's light,
    Serene visage flight.

Sinai, South Dakota. *The days pass swiftly for life here on earth, not only for humankind but for animals and plants as well — as for a tulip blossom during the short and urgent springtime of the North — since all of creation has been subjected to the thralldom of decay. Once sin entered into the affairs of the creation through Adam and Eve's first mishap, longevity has been greatly reduced, and creation sighs and suffers for release from this captivity.*

VOLUME 7. Time and Space, Awesome Teachers 39

40 JOURNEYS THROUGH PRAIRIE AND FOREST Poetic Essays On The Big Questions of Life

Passing of Time

Fleeting Is Time

Time, fleeting as a weaver's shuttle, lost amongst the vapors of noonday,
Solemnly sweeping along rough rapids in ever-increasing vortices,
Silently surrendering my exploits and visions in compromising futility,
Addressing this well-lit heart with kind but firm messages:
Time has no mercy indeed.
But for this man's station I shall ever fight boldly the fight
Of keeping my candle lit to the very end of this too-short mission.

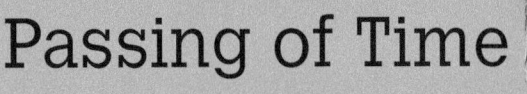

Florissant, Colorado. *The earth has experienced many upheavals over the course of history, some of which have covered ancient forests with sediments and water that led to their petrification. Millennia have passed sine this tree was covered, and it has been unearthed by powerful erosive forces, showing how the passing of time can affect all things in nature.*

Ecuador. *The earth was once an Eden ... or at least a part of it where Adam and Eve resided before they sinned and fell from perfection. Nowadays we see the evidence of great tectonic forces that have ruptured the planet's surface and created great mountains through block faulting or folding, and in some cases by volcanic activity, from previously flat terrain, as evidenced by sedimentary rocks at the tops of these great edifices. What changes time has wrought!*

Passing of Time

Life — So Short

This life, so short, so quickly gone
Reveals few traces of my song,
In world's great pageant, eons spent,
A tiny bit that came and went.

And yet I know tis not in vain,
That God might draw me through this strain;
There lie great reasons I am here,
Yet when shall they be bright and clear?

Life's Passing

So quickly, so very quickly move along the days of life's splendor,
No sooner begun than passing away as a fading flower.
Too soon, too soon the blossoms spring up,
    flourish, and then die in the summer's heat.
Tears shed for lost days can never be redeemed,
Nor can one's sorrow for wasted opportunities be quenched.
Days come, days go: birth, life, death — so quickly runs the course.
Let not the course be run in vain,
    but let it ever race swiftly towards consummate dreams,
Visions of that wonderful world to soon regenerate the earth,
A world of life abundant and never-ending pleasures!

Passing of Time

chapter 8

Live Today!

Live today to its fullest,
For you know not what tomorrow will bring.
Though your life is directed from above,
And your hopes may fall into sore trouble,
Recall your glorious end
If but patience and love rule throughout your fleeting days.

Porter, Minnesota. *Fragrant purple phlox surround an aging house, where pioneer inhabitants are long gone, mere memories of the past now shrouded by the gorgeous regeneration of the beauty and infinite complexity of the creation... whose design is timeless.*

Chapter 9 Use of Time

No Time to Waste

Of all things in this world I hate,
Cruel laziness ranks very high:
To master not the time of fate,
Be captive to the masses sly …

Which lurk in prisons of disgrace,
Approving sluggish lethargy;
Oh, such ill passion chills my face,
Destroys all hope of spirits free.

I cannot bear the thought of crime
So costly as the waste of time.
Console me, soul, no jot or tittle,
That I might not accomplish little.

Galapagos Islands, Ecuador. *These sleeping iguanas seem to care little for managing their time, so much like many people who fritter away their days without recognizing that time is their most important possession.*

Chapter 9 Use of Time

Sunrise, Sunset

Sunrise, sunset, days pass in silent haste,
Flurry of quiet zeal hidden behind furrowed forehead,
Mighty effort of hands and mind laboring for the mastery
Of elusive enterprise, heartfelt dreams, vivid passion …
Life lived so quickly, so intensely — then gone.

Here I rest as one who has run the race,
Though the effort ceases not.
Onward I plunge, as a player obsessed
By unseen visions around the next corner,
The hope of renewed joy beyond the river's bend.

Yes, I have run the race, but though tired
Continue to run and clear all barriers,
Hastening on when objectives seem lost.
Even so, forward, onward … make haste …
For tomorrow I shall be gone — sunrise, sunset.

Then who will raise the call
Of soldier's lonesome quest,
When this dim world shall fall …
And I am heaven's guest?

Pritchett, Texas. *Sunrise, sunset … quickly the days pass, and we suddenly realize how far down the road of life we have passed. The wise use of the time we have, and doing whatever our hands have to do with our might, is a most essential way of serving the great God who made us.*

Fredericksburg, Texas. *No greater use of time can there be but loving one's children, spouse, family, and friends, for they constitute the real stuff of life, those blessings made in the image of Elohim that transcend this life on earth.*

Use of Time

Chapter 9

Time

Flee from time, oh little one;
Rest your fate till you've begun
To fathom hard-fought efforts small,
And probed your life while searchlights call
Above the mediocre crowd,
As later lights will call out loud,
"Recall the past, see far ahead,
Remember life, regard the dead
Who long-since past knew more than you,
And guarded hand-fought secrets few."

My eyes looked up and there I saw,
A Mighty One, disclosed in awe,
Who said, "Dear boy, to grow up tall,
Take heed of time, let it not fall
Among the trash of days ill spent,
For never more shall they come hence."
I listened, but could barely seize
So little of the deep blue breeze
Which drifted through my clouded mind,
And stirred dead leaves I'd left behind.

The leaves were crumpled, dank and gray,
Their scent was faint, yet sweet as hay.
As days wore on they seemed to come
Within my reach; was it wisdom?
I could not tell but pleaded time
Once more to yield her stately shine.
"Were leaves of gray worth sorting through?
Were lessons past designed, though few,
To teach where future steps should lead
So your own wealth might my mouth feed?"

"Be patient boy, you'll someday grow,
Into a man of statue so
Renowned that you yourself will shed
Some falling leaves for sage's beds.
If patience rules your humble crown,
If love and mercy, faith abound,
So nothing less than these, and more,
Within your being fill your store;
Then someday you will find with shock,
That leaves aren't dead, nor lights turned dark,
And fate rests not with chance as some
Bleak minds of past have stumbled from.

"These all, you'll find, have common ends
And common starts, while striving men
Seek glory great in quest for fame
Denying hope from meaner game.
You see, these all have perfect source:
All leaves, all lights, all fame, all course
Derive their strength from One sublime,
Whose greatest gift is use of time."

chapter 10
Take Careful Note of the Beauty Within Your Space

Sinai, South Dakota. *Perhaps no insect on earth is more closely attached to making the most of its time is the honeybee worker. It beats its wings 200 times a second while flying up to 15 miles per hour, and during its five to six week life it visits multiple thousands of flowers to collect nectar and pollen to produce one twelfth of a teaspoon of honey. It never wastes time, and is ever vigilant to defend the hive. Let us learn from these wise creatures of the Creator's making.*

VOLUME 7. Time and Space, Awesome Teachers

Chapter 10
Take Careful Note of the Beauty Within Your Space

The beauty of the creation is an awesome teacher, for as Romans 1:19-20 says, "For whatever is to be known of God is plain to them [those who hinder the Truth by their wickedness]; God Himself has made it plain — for ever since the world was created, His invisible nature, His everlasting power and divine being, have been quite perceptible in what He has made. So they have no excuse" (Moffatt Translation).

Perhaps no other creation on earth rings forth the reality of Elohim's creation than flowers, those reproductive parts of plants that typify the generative power of all creation that is destined to increase endlessly and fill all the earth … and ultimately all of the universe. "Ever wider shall His dominion spread, endlessly at peace: He shall sit on David's throne, to give it lasting foundations of justice and right" (Isaiah 9:7, Knox Translation).

Chapter 10: Take Careful Note of the Beauty Within Your Space

All around us are found the incomparable beauty and fragrance of the creation, especially amongst the flowers with their infinite variety, all pointing to the awesome character of the One who made them, and in whose image people are made. Getting to know that One is the first step in knowing the self.

Take Careful Note of the Beauty Within Your Space

Old Petra Is Gone

That tree that I thought, when a youth, would forever stand, Old Petra, is gone …
The beautiful, spreading, quaking cottonwood,
That gentle, hardy giant of my youthful forested valley
That so encouraged me year after year
With its rugged bark that endured icy winters, insect attacks,
    lightning strikes, and diseases …
Roots reaching creek-ward, the waters bubbling over rocks a stone's throw away.

A sentinel of survival like no other icon of the forested valley
It stood there for over 100 years, keeping watch over the valley of my youth,
The huge edifice a messenger of hope and recovery during my darkest hours,
A helper sent by the great Creator to calm and uplift when worlds came crashing down
Upon the hopes and dreams of a budding son of the Plains,
Ever seeking solace amidst the harshest of life's storms.

But now I sit upon the very site of old Petra's domain …
For he is no more, no, not even a trace.
Only a break above in the forest canopy gives evidence where he once stood.
A lone fledgling elm now stands starkly where once this giant of a tree
Claimed supremacy over all other champions of this fertile valley,
Itself a miracle in the face of the devastating Dutch elm disease.

Yet against all odds the elm stands in the place of the giant cottonwood,
Perhaps paying homage to this lost giant in vain hope that it can preserve its memory,
Snubbing the threats of disease and death to somehow conquer the loss of its mentor …
Maybe even waiting for me to return and see that life goes on despite the age's chaos,
A lowly but firm and healthy elm whose face-off with death is perhaps forthcoming,
But for now laughed at … for what else is a lone elm tree to do?   *Continued on page 59*

Continued from page 58

I looked, thought, and pondered this great debacle,
Of a seemingly invincible tree now totally obliterated from the face of the earth,
Fallen and returned to dust, as must all life find its repose
Within this thin skin of soil upon the land that separates life from death.
Though I was instructed carefully by the great tree in patience, kindness, and love,
The Creator never intended my native-born soul-mate to live forever.

But old Petra was always there, there when I needed him as I grew,
As a reminder of the great handiwork and character of One who made all things.
In his place rises a new tree, one that must fight for its life
Amidst the pain of disease, drought, and competition from surrounding trees ...
But for now it is beautiful and healthy,
Protected for a season for as long as it must live.

I am that new tree, that healthy elm that the Creator has planted there
Where once stood the mighty Petra of my youth.
I am no longer a child, but now a man who looks heavenward towards better things
That the flourishing elm reminds me I must seek.
As the giant cottonwood grew to be a forest patriarch, then faltered, and finally fell,
So I and all flesh will flourish for a season, then falter and fall ... to return to dust.

I am nearing the age of fullness, and will fall and return to the earth ...
But like the great old Petra I am not afraid.
I know of the great brilliance the future holds for those fallen in faith,
In the footsteps of my Elder Brother who created the massive cottonwood of my youth
That taught me so many lessons and nurtured me through trials sore,
And showed the way to the Kingdom on earth when this dust will shed its mortality.

chapter 10

Take Careful Note of the Beauty Within Your Space

Porter Minnesota. *The giant cottonwood tree that graced the valley of the Yellow Medicine River is now gone, not a branch or remnant of it left. A lone elm tree stretches skyward in its place, reminding us that time waits for no one; all life in this age of decay must have an end, but we are promised that the unseen world will someday soon replace this fallen Eden… "Your will be done on earth as it is in heaven." The Creator will not forget His people who rest in the earth, and will raise them up to eternal life, and renew Eden upon the earth.*

www.ingramcontent.com/pod-product-compliance
Lightning Source LLC
Chambersburg PA
CBHW041410160426
42811CB00106B/1614